VEGETARIAN KETO DIET FOR BEGINNERS

A Lifestyle to Lose Weight, Boost Energy, Crush Cravings, and Transform your Life

ANDREA J. CLARK

Disclaimer

This publication contains the opinions and ideas of its author. It is intended to provide helpful and informative material on the subjects addressed in the publication. It is sold with the understanding that the author and the publisher are not engaged in rendering medical, health, or any other kind of personal or professional services in the book. The reader should consult his or her medical, health or other competent professional before adopting any of the suggestions in this book.

The author and publisher are not responsible for the results that come from the application of the content within this book. This applies to risk, loss, personal or otherwise. This also applies to both direct and indirect application of the information contained in this publication.

INTRODUCTION

A lot of people have come to me complaining about the struggles of trying to eat vegetarian diet whilst remaining in ketosis. After all, most of the veggie meals you get offered on restaurant menus or in shops are built around some form of carb. Pasta, bread, rice, legumes, grains, fruit, root vegetables; you name it. You then have the other side of the story with all of the keto diets focused around beef, pork, chicken, or fish. The two just don't seem to go together easily, but they can actually live in perfect harmony if you know the right tips and tricks – all of which will be detailed in the upcoming pages.

So, why keto and vegetarian?

There's a whole host of benefits that the vegetarian diet can offer alone which are only boosted when combined with ketosis. Less animal protein means less risk of extremely life-affecting illnesses such as cardiovascular disease, diabetes, and cancer. Alongside this, the ketogenic diet is going from strength to strength in terms of anecdotal and scientific evidence for weight loss, increased energy, skin health, longevity, and many other benefits. Together, these two diet structures create the perfect approach to eating for health and happiness.

What's in the book?

In this book, we are discussing what is known as *lacto-ovo vegetarian*, meaning a diet including eggs, dairy, and all things vegetarian. Even if you hope to someday become a full vegan, this is a good place to start, as it reduces the changes of nutrient deficiencies.

You'll be learning everything you need to know about the vegetarian ketogenic diet including the benefits, a few tips and tricks to make it easier, and some deliciously easy low carb, high fat vegetarian recipes for your day to day life. These recipes are packed with healthy ingredients, and each recipe comes with detailed nutritional information including calories, fat, carbs and protein.

Why should you read this book?

Everyone struggles to stay in shape and food is one of the trickiest things to get a good grip of. With exercise you may only need to hit the gym 3 or 4 times a week, then the rest of the time you can forget about it. On the other hand, food is an entirely different story. We eat every single day multiple times and each meal, no matter how small it is, can make a massive difference.

Therefore, knowing the truth and some clear-cut guidelines simplifies everything about your eating plan so you know what's good and what you'll want to avoid. This book takes away all the nonsense and strips away the confusion from your health and fitness journey, putting everything in easy to understand information for you to implement right away.

Don't believe me? Well, turn to the next page to find out...

VEGETARIAN KETOGENIC DIET

THE VEGETARIAN DIET

WHY GO VEGETARIAN

Seen as an unconventional diet for many years, vegetarianism has recently been gaining in popularity because of its benefits to human health and for the planet.

Vegetarianism can bring many benefits to your health and wellbeing. It can improve your skin, digestion, mood, and mental health. It can help reduce carbon emissions and promote local industry.

People who consume a vegetarian diet are often seen as fringe eaters that have an unnatural passion for the rights of animals, but a vegetarian diet can be more than that. While a lot of vegetarians do view animal rights passionately, it is important for you to start seeing a vegetarian lifestyle beyond animal rights.

Below are several important reasons why you should go vegetarian:

1. It's better for your health

As far as nutrition goes, people who consume a vegetarian diet will have lower cholesterol levels, and will consume fewer saturated fats that are found in meats. It is also a perfect way to get more phytochemicals, vitamin E and C, antioxidants, folate, potassium, magnesium, and fiber.

2. You will have lower disease risk

Along with the added nutrients, a vegetarian diet will reduce your risk of several diseases. Eating more fruits and veggies will help with eye health and reducing the risk of macular degeneration and cataracts. It will also reduce your risk of breast, colon, and prostate cancer, along with the reduction of blood pressure, cholesterol, and cardiovascular disease.

3. It is eco-friendly

Besides the obvious health benefits of following a vegetarian diet, it also plays an important part in promoting environmental sustainability.

As a matter of fact, rearing farmed animals requires large amount of natural resources, such as grain, land and fresh water. For example, did you know that the water required to rear the meat to create one steak is equivalent to two month's worth of showers? Did you know that 30% of the earth's entire land surface is used for rearing farmed animals?

University of Oxford researchers found that cutting meat products from your diet could reduce an individual's carbon footprint from food by up to 73 per cent.

Just by becoming vegetarian, we can reduce the impact of climate change, rainforest destruction, and pollution.

4. You will save money

Vegetables can be found anywhere with a relatively cheap price. Just by cutting out meat, you can save on your food expenses. Research suggests vegetarians can save at least $4,000 more than meat-eaters per year.

These are some of the most important reasons why we should consume a vegetarian diet. The good news is you can get many of the health benefits of being vegetarian without going all the way. You can start with "Meatless Monday", or start replacing meat with plant-based sources of protein a couple of times a week to start seeing the benefits.

THE KETOGENIC DIET

WHAT IS THE KETOGENIC DIET?

Put quite simply, the ketogenic diet is a high-fat, low carb, moderate protein diet. It is really quite simple. Once you get started on it, you'll find it to be very intuitive.

All human bodies require three main macronutrients to survive: carbohydrates, proteins, and fats. For years, we have been taught that we need to eat a high carb, moderate protein, and low fat diet. But what has that really lead to? High rates of obesity, sickness, and poor health across the board. Eating high carb leads people to go on binges, eating too much, and making themselves sick. What if we change our thinking, and entirely change the focus of our diets?

The keto diet changes the focus from carbs to fat. On a keto diet, you want your intake to be very high-fat, with close to zero carbohydrates. Most keto practitioners eat

80% of their daily calories from fat. So what does that look like?

1 gram of fat has 9 calories. So if you're operating on a 2,000-calorie diet per day, you need 80% of that to come from fat. 80% of 2,000 calories would be 1,600 calories, or 178 grams of fat per day. Don't worry, there isn't this much math involved in day-to-day keto eating!

Okay, but what about the other two macronutrients? On a keto diet, you'll eat 80% fat, 15% protein, and only 5% carbs. Let's continue with our 2,000-calorie example. 1 gram of carbohydrates and protein both have 4 calories. On a 2,000-calorie diet, you'll want 15% to be protein, which works out to 300 calories, or 75 grams of protein. Carbs are even less — 5% of your 2,000 calories. That ends up being only 100 calories, or 25 grams of carbohydrates.

So in a typical keto day, you'll eat 178 grams of fat, 75 grams of protein, and 25 grams of carbohydrates. If you're feeling a bit overwhelmed, don't worry, we're going to do the hard work for you. At the end of this book, we've included a list of recipes and meal suggestions so you can easily stay within these guidelines.

The big takeaway is this: on keto, you get almost all of your daily calories from fats, and reduce your intake of carbohydrates down close to nothing.

THE VEGETARIAN KETOGENIC DIET

Now that you understand what is a vegetarian diet and a ketogenic diet, let's dive right in and take a look at what the combination of both diets can do for you.

WHAT IS THE VEGETARIAN KETOGENIC DIET?

The vegetarian ketogenic diet is a low-carb, high-fat diet that excludes meat. At first glance, the diet may seem difficult to follow because the ketogenic diet requires high fat and low carb; however, it is possible if you make wise dietary choices. First, let's discuss what benefits you will gain by following this diet.

BENEFITS OF THE VEGETARIAN KETOGENIC DIET

You will lose weight

Weight loss is the first and most obvious benefit of the vegetarian ketogenic diet. Because you're eating primarily fat, your body starts to burn fat for energy. That quickly leads to loss of excess fat. You'll watch the inches melt away from your body over the weeks as you commit to keto.

You will gain energy

The next huge benefit comes in the form of energy. Most people usually report an energy boost during the first weeks of the vegetarian ketogenic diet. This energy boost also comes in the form of mental energy. Instead of feeling tired and in need of a coffee after lunch, you would have more energy at work and would be able to stay focused and energetic throughout the day.

You will have better heart health

The benefits of vegetarian keto on your overall health indicators are also impressive. Although many people fear that eating a high-fat diet will lead to high cholesterol, repeated studies have shown the opposite to be true. Those who followed a high-fat diet rich in whole, unprocessed foods, actually came to have lower levels of unhealthy cholesterols. This, in turn, leads to greater heart health and better cardiovascular function. In addition, the vegetarian diet is full of "heart healthy" foods that are high in fiber, and a diet rich in fiber will reduce cholesterol, and keep blood sugar levels low.

You will look younger

Another health benefit of the vegetarian ketogenic diet is its anti-aging properties. So how does this work? Our youthful appearance, youthful body, and youthful brain function all stem from one little part of our cells: mitochondria. Simply put, mitochondria are the factories in our cells that produce energy. When we are young, we have plenty of mitochondria. As we get older, we produce less mitochondria and we have less energy.

The vegetarian ketogenic diet stops this aging process. Studies have actually shown that on a high-fat, low-carb vegetarian diet, our cells not only produce more mitochondria, but they also have more of the antioxidants needed to function properly. This is how the diet actually slows down the visible and invisible effects of aging.

In addition, the vegetarian diet, one high in vegetables, will naturally be also high in water content. This increase in water and nutrients will give you clearer skin, healthier hair, and better functioning of all your internal organs. In other words, it gives your cells the superpower of growth.

You will have reduced risk of Diabetes

There's one more big health benefit of the vegetarian ketogenic diet, and that's fighting against type 2 diabetes.

First of all, let's quickly go over what happens when someone is pre-diabetic. When you eat food, especially carbohydrates, your body turns that food into glucose, which enters the bloodstream and gives you energy.

Some glucose is good for you, but too much is bad. So to control this, the body releases insulin. Insulin tells the liver to store some glucose as fat. All that makes sense, but what happens if we become insensitive to insulin?

When we eat too many carbs, or too much food, insulin can become less effective and as a result, more glucose stays in the blood stream. When this happens, we become "pre-diabetic", meaning we have a high risk of getting diabetes.

How does the vegetarian keto diet help this? With its focus on high-fat, fiber-rich foods, the vegetarian keto diet results in less glucose in the bloodstream. Our food is, instead, being converted into Ketones. So, less glucose in the blood stream, means less need for insulin. Less need for insulin means, you guessed it, less risk for diabetes!

When a person becomes diabetic, their body loses the ability to effectively regulate their blood sugar. This can be pretty scary, especially for someone who has never paid attention to their nutrition before. Diabetic people can still eat carbs, but they must balance it with painful and often expensive insulin injections.

The vegetarian keto diet can help to manage diabetes, in the same way that it helps prevent it. By eating foods high in fats, the body produces Ketones instead of glucose. This keeps blood glucose levels more stable, and is a much safer situation for people with diabetes.

You will have reduced risk of Alzheimer's

Now let's turn to Alzheimer's. This disease, which has exploded into our collective conscience in the last century, is frightening for all of us. Alzheimer's is a degenerative disease that eats away at the brain, removing memory and causing pain to the sick person and their family. Luckily, there is good news. Recent research shows that the vegetarian keto diet may help to prevent and heal Alzheimer's.

How? Well, it actually comes from Alzheimer's similarity to Diabetes. During Alzheimer's, brain cells experience a form of insulin resistance. Over many years of being exposed to so much insulin, the brain cells wear down. Obviously, Alzheimer's is much more complicated than this, but let's keep it simple.

By reducing the amount of insulin in your bloodstream over an extended period of time, the vegetarian keto diet can help to prevent and even to reverse the effects of Alzheimer's.

Research has also indicated that meat eaters have 2-3 times the risk of developing Alzheimer's, compared to those who consume a vegetarian diet.

You will have reduced risk of cancer

Okay, but what about that dreaded disease, cancer? How does a vegetarian ketogenic diet help prevent or protect against cancer?

Most of us have either experienced it first hand, or had someone we know and love experience cancer. It seems to only be growing in power, and while the scientists work on a cure for good, it turns out that vegetarian ketogenic diet can help us fight cancer using only the strength of our diet.

A low-carb diet fights cancer cells by starving them of food and energy. How does this work? It turns out that cancer cells feed off of glucose, or blood sugar. So, by reducing the amount of glucose in the blood stream, we are able to starve the cancer cells, slowing down or preventing their growth.

Furthermore, the healing properties of fruits and vegetables have long been celebrated, especially where cancer is concerned. These foods are very high in nutrients and minerals, but lower in calories. Berries, for example, are high in anti-oxidants, compounds well known for their ability to fight oxidation in the body, and oxidation can lead to cancer. So, by increasing the amount of vegetables and fruits in the diet, you give your body the tools it needs to fight cancer.

The Takeaway

Different nutrients have different health benefits, so by eating a well-rounded vegetarian ketogenic diet, you will naturally be getting more nutrients than a diet of processed foods and meat products. This will in turn lead to a whole host of benefits such as improved muscle function, boosted moods, mental clarity, and increased energy. It takes time and patience to feel all these benefits, but they are out there, just waiting for you to feel them.

So, how can you begin to reap all the health benefits of a

vegetarian ketogenic diet? Begin slowly, and take some time to do your research. In this book, you will find many vegetarian ketogenic recipes that will help you get started. After that, you can do more research and make a meal plan that suits your needs and personal schedule.

WHAT TO EAT ON A VEGETARIAN KETOGENIC DIET

Here's what you CAN eat:

- Berries such as raspberries, blackberries and blueberries.
- Leafy greens such as spinach and kale.
- Plant-based fats such as coconut oil, olive oil, and MCT oil.
- Eggs and dairy such as hard cheeses, heavy cream and butter.
- Dairy alternatives such as coconut milk, almond milk, coconut cream, and vegan cheeses.
- Plant-based protein such as tempeh, tofu and seitan.
- Low carb vegetables such as broccoli, cauliflower, zucchini and avocado.
- Nuts and seeds such as pistachios, almonds, sunflower seeds, and pumpkin seeds.
- Sweeteners such as stevia, erythritol or other low-carb sweeteners.

Here's what you CAN'T eat:

- Meat, fish and poultry.
- Grains such as wheat, corn, rice and cereal.
- Bread and Pasta.
- High-carb vegetables such as corn, sweet potatoes, potatoes and yam.
- Legumes such as lentils, black beans and peas.
- High-carb fruit such as apples, bananas and oranges.
- Sugar such as honey, agave, and maple syrup.

FIVE EASY STEPS TO GO VEGETARIAN KETO

Getting ready to go vegetarian keto may seem like an intimidating task, but with the right preparation, it doesn't need to be. The diet is a big change from the Standard American Diet, but if you come into it with the right tools and the right mentality, you will be astounded by what you can achieve. Here are five easy steps to start your vegetarian keto diet journey:

1. HAVING THE RIGHT MINDSET

Being in the right state of mind when you begin the vegetarian ketogenic diet can mean the difference between failure and success. One of the best things you can do is switch your thinking from long-term to short-term. Of course, you have long-term goals, but if you only focus on the long-term, things can feel overwhelming. Instead, try setting more immediate short-term goals to help you get through the transition period.

For example, if you begin your vegetarian ketogenic diet

thinking "*I can never eat carbs again!*" you might feel like this is impossible. But if instead, you think "*I am going to take a break from carbs for one month.*" Well, that seems easier.

Make the commitment to follow a strict vegetarian ketogenic diet for just one month before you take your first cheat day. You will see the beginning of your incredible results.

The other aspect of your mentality that you need to be ready for is cravings. Cravings are a totally normal and natural part of every diet. At some point during that first month, you will feel cravings for carbs.

There are two things you can do to overcome these cravings. The first is more to remind yourself that cravings will get less intense over time. If you can commit to that first month, you will feel your cravings decrease significantly.

The second thing that you can do is tell yourself: "*You don't need to eat carbs now. You'll feel better tomorrow.*" This might actually help to relieve the mental stress of cravings. Tell yourself you can think about it again tomorrow, and then do something to distract yourself. Have high-fat snacks available for when you get hungry, and have your mental defenses ready to defeat the cravings.

2. PREPARING YOUR KITCHEN

Another essential step in preparing to go vegetarian keto is getting your kitchen in order. If you try to be on the vegetarian ketogenic diet but your kitchen is full of bread, pasta, and processed foods, you're going to give in to your cravings immediately. Once you've decided to commit to the diet, you should take a few days to prepare your kitchen. Get rid of craving foods, processed foods, and all the foods that don't fit within the diet.

So, what food should you have in your kitchen?

At least at the beginning of your vegetarian ketogenic journey, make sure to keep it simple. Don't try to make fancy, low-carb bread or crackers, and stay away from keto desserts. Fill your refrigerator with vegetables and keto-approved cheeses. Learn how to make three or four quick and easy vegetarian keto meals, such as the ones found at the end of this book, and mentally prepare yourself to eat those during the first weeks.

Keeping it simple will help you avoid the intense cravings of the first week. Having the right ingredients on hand will help you stay on keto, and not resort to eating high carb snacks that could kick you out of Ketosis.

3. BE PREPARED FOR THOSE FIRST WEEKS

The first days and weeks of the ketogenic diet are some of the hardest that you'll go through. That's why taking steps like preparing your mindset and supplying your kitchen are so important. If you have the right tools in place, you'll be able to get through those first difficult days.

During the first weeks of keto, your body and mind will go through many changes. You'll lose weight but then plateau. You'll feel angry, hungry, tired, and frustrated. Don't give up! We've all been there; we've all struggled through these days. If you can get through these days and stick to the diet, you'll soon find yourself in a better place than ever before.

4. DEALING WITH THE KETO FLU

The keto flu is a nickname for the physical changes that your body goes through when you first give up on carbohydrates. Because you're going without carbohydrates probably for the first time, your body might react poorly. Common symptoms of the keto flu are headaches, nausea, fatigue, and other uncomfortable physical reactions.

As a caveat, not everyone experiences the keto flu, and there are varying degrees of intensity. You might find your head in a fog for a few days. You may feel tired, or you may feel extremely sick. Whatever happens, as long as it isn't dangerous to your overall well-being, just know that this is part of the withdrawal after a lifetime of eating overly-processed unhealthy carbohydrates.

If your current diet is relatively healthy, but heavily focused on carbohydrates, then you shouldn't experience a very extreme version of the keto-flu. However, if you are currently eating a diet of highly processed food, refined sugars, box cereals, prepackaged foods, and sodas, then you may want to consider slowly bringing yourself into keto.

Gradually reduce your carbohydrate consumption over 4 to 6 weeks before switching fully to keto. This can prevent the extreme symptoms of the keto flu. Once the keto flu symptoms start to hit, the best thing you can do is increase your salt and fluid intake by drinking cups of bouillon.

Most of all, if you feel yourself getting sick and uncomfortable during the first weeks of keto, don't panic! Know that this is normal, and if you want support to get through it, there are plenty of online communities full of people who want to help you get the most out of keto.

5. CONTROLLING THOSE SUGAR CRAVINGS

No doubt about it, you will be plagued by cravings for sugar during those first few weeks on keto. Especially when you get hungry or need a snack, the desire to eat some bread, cake, or cookies will be strong.

Luckily, there are ways to beat these cravings. The best way to overcome cravings is by being prepared. Pay attention to your body's cycles. What time do you normally get hungry? If you have a long day ahead of you, and you know it'll be a big stretch between meals, bring a high-fat snack with you. In fact, having high-fat snacks on hand can make all the difference between overcoming cravings, and giving into them.

Some high-fat, keto-approved snacks to carry around with you are natural, low-carb peanut butter with carrots, unprocessed cheeses or dark chocolate. Having those on hand will prevent you from heading to the nearest vending machine and ruining your diet.

Now, let's look at the dos and don'ts of the vegetarian ketogenic diet:

DOS

- Eliminate all animal flesh from your diet.
- Limit your total carbohydrate consumption.
- Get at least 80% of your calories from fat.
- Eat plenty of low-carb vegetables such as leafy greens, zucchini, cauliflower and broccoli.
- Consume around 15% of your calories from eggs, dairy and plant-based proteins.
- Supplement with nutrients that you may not be getting enough of like vitamins D3, DHA & EPA, iron, and zinc.

DON'TS

- Consume packaged vegetarian meat substitutes.
- Consume any genetically modified products.

THE TAKEAWAY

The biggest thing you need to prepare before you start your vegetarian keto journey is your mentality. Getting mentally prepared for the hardships and cravings that you will face during those first days and weeks will help you stick with the diet. Prepare your pantry by eliminating all non-vegetarian keto foods, and prepare your mind by reminding yourself of your ultimate goal: your weight loss and your healthy lifestyle!

AMAZING VEGETARIAN KETO RECIPES

THE BASICS

CAULIFLOWER RICE

Serves: 4

Prep time: 5 min

Cook time: 8 min

Ingredients:

- 1 large head cauliflower
- 1 tbsp olive oil or butter
- Pinch of salt

Directions:

1. Cut the cauliflower into large pieces: Trim the cauliflower florets, cutting away as much stem as possible.
2. In two or three batches, transfer the cauliflower to a food processor.
3. Pulse until the mixture resembles couscous.

4. Heat a tablespoon of olive oil or butter in a large skillet over medium heat.
5. Add in the cauliflower rice and sprinkle with salt.
6. Cover the skillet and cook for 6 to 8 minutes, until the cauliflower rice is as tender as you like.
7. You can refrigerate the cauliflower rice for up to a week.

Nutrition Facts Per Serving:

- Calories: 42 kcal
- Total Fat: 3.06 g
- Total Carbs: 3.3 g
- Dietary Fiber: 1.3 g
- Net Carbs: 2 g
- Protein: 1.3 g

CAULIFLOWER PIZZA CRUST

Serves: 1 pizza crust

Prep time: 20 min

Cook time: 30 min

Ingredients:

- 1 piece cauliflower head, stalk removed
- ¼ cup Parmesan, grated
- ½ cup mozzarella, shredded
- ½ tsp kosher salt
- ½ tsp oregano, dried
- ¼ tsp garlic powder
- 2 eggs, beaten lightly

Directions:

1. Preheat oven to 400°F (205°C). Use parchment paper to line a baking sheet.

2. Cut the cauliflower head into florets. In a food processor, pulse the cauliflower until fine.

3. Place the cauliflower in a steamer basket. Steam it and drain well. Allow to cool.

4. In a bowl, mix the fine cauliflower together with the Parmesan, mozzarella, salt, oregano, eggs, and garlic powder.

5. Place the mixture in the center of the lined baking sheet and form into a circle to look like a pizza crust.

6. Bake for about 20 minutes.

7. Add your toppings of choice and bake for another 10 minutes.

8. Serve hot. Enjoy.

Nutrition Facts per Serving:

- Calories: 483 kcal
- Total Carbs: 26.1 g
- Dietary Fiber: 6.6 g
- Net Carbs: 19.5 g
- Total Fat: 21.05 g
- Protein: 49.11 g

KETO COCONUT ROSEMARY BREAD

This coconut rosemary bread is a good accompaniment for paleo pates or soups. The bread's lighter texture, coupled with the aromatic rosemary flavor, is great to enjoy during the summers.

Serves: 10

Prep time: 20 min

Cook time: 45 min

Ingredients:

- 4 eggs
- ¼ cup coconut milk
- ¼ cup olive oil
- 1 tsp sea salt
- 1 tsp baking soda
- 1 tsp rosemary, freshly ground
- ¾ cup coconut flour
- ⅓ cup flaxseed meal

Directions:

1. Preheat the oven to 350°F or 175°C.
2. In a large bowl, use a hand mixer to beat the olive oil, eggs, rosemary, and coconut milk. Mix until smooth.
3. Add the baking soda, sea salt, and flaxseed meal. Mix well.
4. Add the coconut flour. Mix well. The mixture should be dry at this point.
5. Use a spatula to scrape off the dough, and pour it into an oven-proof dish. Use your hands to form the dough into a bread shape. You may also scoop the dough into a baking tin, and use your spatula to spread out the dough.
6. Bake for 45 minutes, or until a toothpick that you inserted comes out clean.
7. Remove from oven. Cool and serve.

Nutrition Facts per Serving:

- Calories: 146.40 kcal
- Total Carbs: 3.02g
- Dietary Fiber: 1.85g
- Net Carbs: 1.17g
- Total Fat: 13.06g
- Protein: 4.87g

KETO SESAME BUNS

While the recipe is easy to make, there are certain variables that can affect the outcome. Use the lightest and finest coconut flour, and use Psyllium powder that's fine, not flaky. It is also important not to use table salt. Instead, use Celtic sea salt or Himalayan salt.

Serves: 12

Prep time: 15 min

Cook time: 50 min

Ingredients:

- 1 cup coconut flour
- ½ cup pumpkin seeds
- 1 cup sesame seeds (Reserve ½ cup sesame seeds for toppings.)
- 1 cup hot water
- ½ cup Psyllium powder

- 1 tbsp sea salt
- 8 egg whites
- 1 tsp aluminum-free baking powder

Directions:

1. Preheat oven to 350°F or 175°C.
2. In a large bowl, combine the dry ingredients. Mix well.
3. Place the eggs whites in a blender and beat until very foamy. Add the whites to the dry ingredients. Use a food processor or a spoon to mix well. The dough should be crumbly.
4. Add 1 cup boiling water and continue to stir until you form a smoother dough. The slightly crumbly dough will keep its shape when formed into a bun.
5. Place ½ cup sesame seeds on a plate. Press the buns into the sesame plate so the seeds stick to the top.
6. On a cookie sheet, place one piece of parchment. Place the sesame buns on the parchment paper.
7. For about 50 minutes, bake the buns at 350°F (175°C).
8. Allow the buns to cool inside the oven to achieve extra-crunchy tops.
9. Remove from oven and serve hot.

Nutrition Facts per Serving:

- Calories: 133 kcal

- Total Carbs: 13.5g
- Dietary Fiber: 9.5g
- Net Carbs: 4g
- Total Fat: 6.5g
- Protein: 6.9g

ZOODLES (ZUCCHINI NOODLES)

Serves: 4

Prep time: 5 min

Cook time: 5 min

Ingredients:

- 4 large zucchini

Directions:

1. Wash the Zucchini thoroughly.
2. Cut the Zucchini noodles using a spiralizer, a mandolin slicer or a vegetable peeler.
3. Set aside on paper towels for 10 minutes.
4. Cook the Zucchini noodles by boiling them, sauté them in oil or simmer them in a sauce

Nutrition Facts Per Serving:

- Calories: 3 kcal
- Total Fat: 0.06g
- Total Carbs: 0.5g
- Dietary Fiber: 0.2g
- Net Carbs: 0.3g
- Protein: 0.43g

BREAKFAST RECIPES

AVOCADO COCONUT MILK SHAKE

Serves: 1

Prep time: 5 min

Cook time: 0 min

Ingredients:

- ½ avocado
- ½ cups Unsweetened Coconut Milk
- 5 drops stevia
- 5 Ice Cubes

Directions:

1. Add all the ingredients to the blender.
2. Blend until smooth.

Nutrition Facts Per Serving:

- Calories: 437 kcal

- Total Fat: 43.34g
- Total Carbs: 20.2g
- Dietary Fiber: 9.4g
- Net Carbs: 10.8g
- Protein: 4.76g

BULLETPROOF COFFEE

Serves: 1

Prep time: 5 min

Cook time: 10 min

Ingredients:

- 1 cup water
- 2 tbsp coffee
- 1 tbsp grass fed butter
- 1 tbsp coconut oil
- ¼ tsp vanilla extract

Directions:

1. Brew coffee your preferred way.
2. Add butter and coconut oil to the blender.
3. Pour the coffee into the blender.
4. Add the vanilla extract and blend for 20 seconds.

<u>Nutrition Facts Per Serving:</u>

- Calories: 284 kcal
- Total Fat: 24.43g
- Total Carbs: 0.14g
- Dietary Fiber: 0g
- Net Carbs: 0.14g
- Protein: 16.54g

CREAMY AVOCADO CACAO CHIA SHAKE

Serves: 1

Prep time: 15 min

Cook time: 0 min

Ingredients:

- ½ avocado
- 1 tbsp chia seeds
- ½ oz 70% dark chocolate
- 1 cup unsweetened almond milk
- 5 ice cubes

Directions:

1. Mix the chia seeds with the unsweetened almond milk and wait for 10 minutes.
2. Add all the ingredients to the blender.
3. Blend until smooth.
4. Topped with some chopped dark chocolate.

<u>Nutrition Facts Per Serving:</u>

- Calories: 533 kcal
- Total Fat: 37.5g
- Total Carbs: 38.72g
- Dietary Fiber: 18.1g
- Net Carbs: 20.62g
- Protein: 15.5g

GREEK YOGURT AND BERRY PARFAIT

Serves: 2

Prep time: 30 min

Cook time: 0 min

Ingredients:

- 1 cup fall-fat unsweetened Greek yogurt
- ⅓ cup mixed frozen berries, crushed
- ⅓ cup chia seeds
- ½ cup unsweetened coconut milk
- 1 tbsp powdered Erythritol
- ¼ tsp ground cinnamon

Directions:

1. In a bowl, mix chia seeds, coconut milk and Erythritol. Leave for at least 30 minutes.
2. In a glass cup, layer the chia pudding, crush berries and yogurt.

3. Top with cinnamon and serve.

Nutrition Facts Per Serving:

- Calories: 382 kcal
- Total Fat: 23.5 g
- Total Carbs: 29.8g
- Dietary Fiber: 12.6g
- Net Carbs: 17.2g
- Protein: 17.56 g

KETO CREAM CHEESE PANCAKE

Serves: 1

Prep time: 5 min

Cook time: 10 min

Ingredients:

- 2 eggs
- 2 oz. cream cheese
- 1 tbsp coconut flour
- ½ tsp cinnamon
- 1 packet stevia

Directions:

1. Beat or blend together the ingredients until the batter is smooth and free of lumps.
2. Two pancakes is equivalent to one serving. On medium-high, heat up a non-stick skillet or pan with coconut oil or salted butter.

3. Ladle the batter on to the pan. Heat until bubbles begin to form on top. Flip over, and cook until the other side is sufficiently browned.
4. Serve. Top with sugar-free maple syrup and grass-fed butter.

Nutrition Facts per Serving:

- Calories: 299 kcal
- Total Fat: 24.6 g
- Total Carbs: 4.2 g
- Dietary Fiber: 0.9 g
- Net Carbs: 3.3 g
- Protein: 15.2 g

MIXED BERRY SMOOTHIE BOWL

Serves: 2

Prep time: 5 min

Cook time: 0 min

Ingredients:

- 1 cup coconut milk
- 2 tbsp peanut butter
- 1 cup frozen mixed berries
- 2 tbsp walnuts
- 1 tbsp chia seeds
- ½ tsp vanilla extract

Directions:

1. Blend coconut milk, peanut butter, frozen berries and vanilla extract until smooth.
2. Top with nuts, chia seeds and some berries.
3. Enjoy!

Nutrition Facts Per Serving:

- Calories: 447 kcal
- Total Fat: 38.8 g
- Total Carbs: 23.8g
- Dietary Fiber: 8g
- Net Carbs: 15.8g
- Protein: 7.24g

PEANUT BUTTER CHIA PUDDING

Serves: 1

Prep time: 3 hrs

Cook time: 0 min

Ingredients:

- 1 tbsp chia seeds
- 1 cup unsweetened almond milk
- ½ tsp ground cinnamon
- 1 tbsp peanut butter
- 8 drops stevia

Directions:

1. Add almond milk, peanut butter, cinnamon and stevia to your blender.
2. Blend until smooth.
3. Add chia seeds to the mixture and stir.
4. Refrigerate for about 3 hours.

5. Enjoy!

Nutrition Facts Per Serving:

- Calories: 384 kcal
- Total Fat: 24.7g
- Total Carbs: 28.17g
- Dietary Fiber: 11.5g
- Net Carbs: 16.7g
- Protein: 16.28g

SPINACH AND MUSHROOM BREAKFAST CASSEROLE

Serves: 8

Prep time: 15 min

Cook time: 40 min

Ingredients:

- 12 oz fresh baby spinach
- ½ lb. mushrooms, sliced
- 1 medium yellow onion, chopped
- 2 cloves garlic, minced
- 6 eggs, beaten
- 5 tbsp unsalted butter
- 16 oz. cottage cheese
- 12 oz. cheddar cheese grated
- Salt and pepper to taste

Directions:

1. Preheat the oven to 350°F.

2. Grease a baking dish with 1 tablespoon butter.
3. In a large skillet, heat the remaining butter over medium heat.
4. Sauté onions, garlic, mushrooms for 3-4 minutes.
5. Add spinach and sauté, until spinach wilt.
6. In a bowl, combine eggs, cheddar cheese, cottage cheese, salt and pepper and mix well. Pour in spinach and mushroom mixture.
7. Pour the mixture into baking dish, and bake for 40 minutes, or until top is golden brown.

Nutrition Facts Per Serving:

- Calories: 431kcal
- Total Fat: 26.4g
- Total Carbs: 27.4g
- Dietary Fiber: 4.5g
- Net Carbs: 22.9g
- Protein: 25.2g

LUNCH RECIPES

ASIAN TOFU SALAD WITH PEANUT BUTTER DRESSING

Serves: 4

Prep time: 20 min

Cook time: 10 min

Ingredients:

- ½ cup smooth peanut butter
- 2 tbsp soy sauce
- 1 tsp hot sauce
- Juice of 1/2 lime
- 2 tbsp water
- 1 cup spinach
- 1 cup carrots, grated
- 1 cup red cabbage, thinly sliced
- 1 lb. extra firm tofu cubes, baked
- ½ cup roasted peanuts
- A bunch of fresh cilantro leaves, for garnish

Directions:

1. In a small bowl, whisk together peanut butter, soy sauce, hot sauce, lime juice and water.
2. In a large salad bowl, add veggies and tofu. Add the dressing and toss to combine.
3. Top with cilantro and peanuts and serve immediately.

Nutrition Facts Per Serving:

- Calories: 438 kcal
- Total Fat: 29.4g
- Total Carbs: 25g
- Dietary Fiber: 5.5g
- Net Carbs: 19.5g
- Protein: 26.6g

AVOCADO TEMPEH SALAD

Serves: 4

Prep time: 10 min

Cook time: 10 min

Ingredients:

- 8 oz. tempeh, cut into thin strips
- 5 tbsp olive oil, divided
- 1 tomato, sliced
- ½ cucumber, chopped
- 1 avocado, cubed
- 2 oz. feta cheese, crumbled
- 1 tbsp apple cider vinegar
- Salt and pepper to taste

Directions:

1. In a frying pan, heat 3 tbsp of olive oil over medium heat.

2. Add tempeh into the pan and cook until the both sides are golden brown.
3. In a large salad bowl, add 2 tbsp of olive oil, apple cider vinegar, salt and pepper.
4. Add tomato, cucumber, avocado, feta and toss to combine.
5. Top with fried tempeh and serve.

Nutrition Facts Per Serving:

- Calories: 386 kcal
- Total Fat: 33.4g
- Total Carbs: 12.4g
- Dietary Fiber: 3.8g
- Net Carbs: 8.6g
- Protein: 13.9g

BROCCOLI, WALNUT AND FETA SALAD

Serves: 4

Prep time: 5 min

Cook time: 5 min

Ingredients:

- 1 head broccoli, cut into florets
- 2 tbsp olive oil
- Juice of ½ lemon
- ¼ cup walnuts
- 2 oz. feta cheese, crumbled
- Salt and pepper to taste

Directions:

1. Steam the broccoli in a microwave. Let cool slightly.
2. In a large serving bowl, place the broccoli,

walnuts and feta cheese. Add olive oil, lemon juice, salt and pepper.

3. Stir to combine.
4. Serve.

Nutrition Facts Per Serving:

- Calories: 151 kcal
- Total Fat: 13.3 g
- Total Carbs: 5.6 g
- Dietary Fiber: 0.5 g
- Net Carbs: 5.1 g
- Protein: 8.2 g

CAPRESE SALAD

Serves: 1

Prep time: 10 min

Cook time: 0 min

Ingredients:

- 2 tomatoes, sliced
- ¼ cups fresh basil leaves
- 1 large ball of Mozzarella, sliced
- 3 tbsp olive oil
- Sea salt and black pepper to taste

Directions:

1. In a serving plate, layer the tomatoes, mozzarella and basil.
2. Drizzle with olive oil and sprinkle with salt and black pepper.
3. Enjoy!

Nutrition Facts Per Serving:

- Calories: 387 kcal
- Total Fat: 41.1g
- Total Carbs: 5.7g
- Dietary Fiber: 1.2g
- Net Carbs: 4.5g
- Protein: 1.2g

CAULIFLOWER MAC & CHEESE

Serves: 4

Prep time: 5 min

Cook time: 25 min

Ingredients:

- 1 large head cauliflower, cut into small florets
- 2 tbsp butter
- 2 tsp olive oil
- ½ cup heavy whipping cream
- 4 oz cream cheese, cubed
- 1 and ½ cup shredded cheddar cheese, divided
- 1 tsp Dijon mustard
- ½ tsp garlic powder
- Salt and pepper to taste

Directions:

1. Heat 2 tsp olive oil on a skillet over medium heat and preheat the oven to 425°F or 220°C.
2. Add cauliflower to the skillet and cook for 5 minutes.
3. Transfer the cauliflower to the baking dish and set aside.
4. For the cheese sauce, combine butter, Dijon mustard, heavy cream and 1 cup cheddar cheese in a medium saucepan. Cook on low heat until everything is melted. Use a whisk to stir in the cream cheese and mix until smooth, and then stir and season with salt, pepper and garlic powder.
5. Pour the cheese sauce over the cauliflower, and stir to combine.
6. Top with the remaining ½ cup cheese and bake until browned, about 15 minutes.
7. Serve.

Nutrition Facts Per Serving:

- Calories: 434 kcal
- Total Fat: 39.11g
- Total Carbs: 6.81g
- Dietary Fiber: 1.6g
- Net Carbs: 5.21g
- Protein: 15.81g

CREAMY ZUCCHINI NOODLES

Serves: 4

Prep time: 10 min

Cook time: 10 min

Ingredients:

- 4 medium zucchini, cut into noodles
- 4 cloves garlic, minced
- 4 tbsp olive oil
- 1 cup heavy cream
- 1 cup fresh basil leaves
- 2 oz. Parmesan cheese, grated
- Salt and black pepper to taste
- For topping: Pine nuts and cherry tomatoes

Directions:

1. In a frying pan, heat olive oil over medium heat.
2. Add garlic and sauté 2 minutes or until fragrant.

3. Add the zucchini noodles and cook about 3-4 minutes.
4. Pour the heavy cream over and stir well.
5. Turn the heat off. Stir in basil leaves.
6. Add salt and pepper.
7. Top with pine nuts, cherry tomatoes and grated Parmesan cheese. Serve.

Nutrition Facts Per Serving:

- Calories: 294 kcal
- Total Fat: 28.7g
- Total Carbs: 5.2g
- Dietary Fiber: 0.4g
- Net Carbs: 4.8g
- Protein: 5.37g

GOAT CHEESE OMELET

Serves: 4

Prep time: 15 min

Cook time: 15 min

Ingredients:

- 8 large eggs
- 2 tbsp butter
- 2 tsp olive oil
- 1 tsp Dijon mustard
- 6 cups spinach
- 8 oz goat cheese
- 4 tbsp heavy cream
- ¼ cup scallions, chopped
- Ground pepper and salt to taste

Directions:

1. In a pan, heat 2 teaspoon of olive oil.

2. Add the spinach and sauté for one to two minutes. Add the mustard, pepper, and salt.
3. Remove vegetables from the pan. Set aside.
4. Mix 8 large eggs, cream, salt, and pepper in a large bowl.
5. Melt butter in a large pan over medium-low heat.
6. Pour egg mixture into the pan and cook for about one minute. You may need to cook in 2 or more batches.
7. Spoon spinach and crumble goat cheese over the eggs.
8. Cook for another 2-3 minutes.
9. Fold the omelet.
10. Garnish with the scallions.

Nutrition Facts Per Serving:

- Calories: 506 kcal
- Total Fat: 43.01g
- Total Carbs: 6.1g
- Dietary Fiber: 1.4g
- Net Carbs: 4.7g
- Protein: 24.74g

GREEK BRIAM WITH FETA

Serves: 4

Prep time: 10 min

Cook time: 25 min

Ingredients:

- 1 white onion, diced
- 3 cloves garlic, minced
- ¼ cup butter
- 4 tbsp olive oil
- ½ cup vegetable stock
- 1 eggplant, diced
- 1 cup cauliflower, chopped
- 4 medium tomatoes, chopped
- 3 zucchini, sliced
- 8 oz. feta cheese, crumbled
- 1 tbsp dried oregano
- ¼ cup parsley, chopped
- Salt and black pepper to taste

Directions:

1. In a large casserole dish, heat butter over medium heat.
2. Cook onions and garlic until fragrant.
3. Add the eggplant and cook for 3 minutes.
4. Next, add cauliflower. Cover with a lid and cook on low for 4-5 minutes.
5. Add tomatoes, zucchini, vegetable stock and cook for another 10 minutes until the vegetables are soft. Stir occasionally.
6. Add dried oregano, top with feta and broil for 5 minutes in oven.
7. Serve with parsley and olive oil.

Nutrition Facts Per Serving:

- Calories: 462 kcal
- Total Fat: 38.01g
- Total Carbs: 22.1g
- Dietary Fiber: 7.2g
- Net Carbs: 14.9g
- Protein: 12.4g

SPINACH AND LEEK QUICHE

Serves: 4

Prep time: 15 min

Cook time: 25 min

Ingredients:

- 1 tbsp olive oil
- 4 cups spinach, chopped
- 2 medium-sized leeks, sliced
- 8 large eggs
- 1 cup grated cheddar cheese
- Salt and pepper, to taste

Directions:

1. Preheat oven to 320°F. Grease a baking dish with cooking spray.
2. In a frying pan, heat olive oil over medium heat.

3. Add spinach and leeks, and sauté for 5-6 minutes, or until the leeks are transparent.
4. In a large bowl, beat the eggs. Add the vegetables, cheddar cheese, salt and pepper in the bowl and mix well.
5. Add the mixture into the baking dish. Bake for 15 minutes.
6. Let cool and serve.

Nutrition Facts Per Serving:

- Calories: 293 kcal
- Total Fat: 22.2g
- Total Carbs: 10.1g
- Dietary Fiber: 1.7g
- Net Carbs: 8.4g
- Protein: 16.4g

SPAGHETTI SQUASH BURRITO BOWLS

Serves: 4

Prep time: 20 min

Cook time: 50 min

Ingredients:

- 2 medium spaghetti squash, halved and seeds removed
- 2 tbsp olive oil
- 1 red onion, sliced
- 1 clove garlic, minced
- 1 red bell pepper, sliced
- 2 jalapenos, cored and sliced
- 1 cup shredded cheddar
- 1 tsp cumin
- 1 tsp chili powder
- 1 small jar of salsa
- 6 green onions, chopped
- ½ cup fresh cilantro, finely chopped

- Salt & pepper to taste

Directions:

1. Preheat the oven to 400°F or 200°C and line a baking sheet with parchment paper.
2. On the baking sheet, drizzle the halved spaghetti squash with olive oil and season with freshly ground black pepper and salt.
3. Place each half face down on the baking sheet.
4. Roast in the oven for 30-45 minutes, until the squash is easily pierced through with a fork.
5. Meanwhile, heat oil in a large pan over medium heat.
6. Sauté the red onion for a few minutes until tender.
7. Add the garlic, cumin and chili powder and cook for another 3-5 minutes.
8. Add the bell peppers and jalapeño, and cook until desired softness. Season with salt and pepper.
9. Remove squash from oven and let cool for 10 minutes.
10. Use a fork to separate and fluff up the flesh of the spaghetti squash and scrape about ½ of the inside out onto a dish.
11. Add the filling to each "bowl" and top with chopped green onions, salsa and shredded cheese.
12. Broil in the oven for 5 minutes, or until cheese is bubble and golden brown.
13. Garnish the bowls with chopped cilantro. Serve.

Nutrition Facts Per Serving:

- Calories: 317 kcal
- Total Fat: 19.8g
- Total Carbs: 27.5g
- Dietary Fiber: 7.5g
- Net Carbs: 20g
- Protein: 12.1g

LOW-CARB MARGHERITA PIZZA

Serves: Makes a 12" pizza with 6 slices

Prep time: 10 min

Cook time: 25 min

Ingredients:

Low Carb Pizza Crust

- 4 tbsp almond flour
- 3 tbsp coconut flour
- 1 cup shredded mozzarella cheese
- 1 egg
- 1 tsp salt

Pizza Toppings

- ¼ cup pizza sauce
- 6 oz mozzarella cheese, sliced
- ½ tsp garlic powder
- ½ tsp dry oregano

- A handful of fresh basil
- 6-10 pitted black olives
- 1 tbsp olive oil

Directions:

1. Preheat oven to 400°F.
2. In a microwave-safe bowl, melt shredded cheese in microwave.
3. Once the cheese is soft, add almond flour, coconut flour, egg and salt and combine to form the dough.
4. Use two sheets of parchment paper to form the dough into the round shape.
5. Bake for 12 minutes or until slightly golden.
6. When the crust is done, add the pizza sauce and spread evenly over the crust.
7. Next, add the mozzarella cheese, oregano, basil, and olives.
8. Bake for another 10 minutes until the cheese is melted.
9. Add olive oil and serve.

Nutrition Facts Per Serving:

- Calories: 126 kcal
- Total Fat: 4.9g
- Total Carbs: 3.7g
- Dietary Fiber: 1.5g
- Net Carbs: 2.2g
- Protein: 17g

TOFU AND ASPARAGUS STIR FRY

Serves: 2

Prep time: 5 min

Cook time: 10 min

Ingredients:

- 1 tbsp olive oil
- 1 small onion, sliced
- 10 oz. firm tofu, drained and cut into cubes
- 2 cloves garlic, minced
- 1 tbsp soy sauce
- 2 cups asparagus, ends trimmed and cut into 2-inch pieces

Directions:

1. Heat oil in a frying pan over high heat.
2. Sauté the tofu until slightly golden.

3. Next, add onions and asparagus and cook for 3 minutes.
4. Add garlic and cook 2 more minutes.
5. Add the soy sauce and stir to combine.
6. Serve.

Nutrition Facts Per Serving:

- Calories: 257 kcal
- Total Fat: 16.7g
- Total Carbs: 14.2g
- Dietary Fiber: 4.2g
- Net Carbs: 10g
- Protein: 18.1g

THAI TOFU SALAD

Serves: 2

Prep time: 15 min

Cook time: 0 min

Ingredients:

- 4 carrots, ribboned with vegetable peeler
- 2 zucchini, ribboned with vegetable peeler
- ½ cup firm tofu, drained and cubed
- 2 tbsp tamarind sauce
- 2 tbsp soy sauce
- 1 tbsp water
- Juice of 1 lime
- 2 tsp Asian chili sauce
- Toppings: lime wedges, crushed peanuts, sriracha, cilantro

Directions:

1. In a large bowl, whisk tamarind sauce, soy sauce, lime juice, water and Asian chili sauce together.
2. Add ribboned carrots, zucchini and tofu. Toss to combine.
3. Serve and top with desired toppings.

Nutrition Facts Per Serving:

- Calories: 159 kcal
- Total Fat: 5.9g
- Total Carbs: 21.2g
- Dietary Fiber: 5.2g
- Net Carbs: 16g
- Protein: 8.24g

VEGETARIAN KETO CLUB SALAD

Serves: 4

Prep time: 10 min

Cook time: 0 min

Ingredients:

- 4 cups romaine lettuce, cut into pieces
- ½ cup cherry tomatoes, halved
- 1 cucumber, diced
- 4 hard boiled eggs, sliced
- 4 oz. cheddar cheese, cubed
- 2 tbsp sour cream
- 2 tbsp mayonnaise
- 1 tbsp dijon mustard
- ½ tsp garlic powder
- ½ tsp onion powder

Directions:

1. Mix the sour cream, Dijon mustard, and mayonnaise. Set aside.
2. In a salad bowl, combine the romaine lettuce, cucumber and tomatoes.
3. Pour the dressing over the salad, and then toss to coat.
4. Top with eggs and cheese. Serve.

Nutrition Facts Per Serving:

- Calories: 244 kcal
- Total Fat: 18.3g
- Total Carbs: 5.14g
- Dietary Fiber: 1.7g
- Net Carbs: 3.44g
- Protein: 14.9g

DINNER RECIPES

ASPARAGUS AND TOMATO FRITTATA

Serves: 4

Prep time: 10 min

Cook time: 15 min

Ingredients:

- 6 oz. fresh asparagus, cut into 1 1/2 inches pieces
- 1 tbsp olive oil
- ½ cup cherry tomatoes, halved
- 1 tsp. dried dill weed
- 4 oz. shredded Monterey Jack
- 6 eggs, beaten in a bowl
- Salt and pepper to taste
- Sliced green onions for garnish

Directions:

1. In a large frying pan, heat oil over medium heat.
2. Add asparagus and cook 3-4 minutes.

3. Next, add tomatoes and dill weed and sauté for 2 minutes.
4. Pour the eggs over the vegetables, and season with salt and black pepper.
5. Sprinkle the cheese over the top.
6. Cook on low for about 6 minutes.
7. Garnish with green onions and serve.

Nutrition Facts Per Serving:

- Calories: 241 kcal
- Total Fat: 18.3g
- Total Carbs: 2.9g
- Dietary Fiber: 1g
- Net Carbs: 1.9g
- Protein: 16.25g

CAULIFLOWER FRIED RICE

Serves: 4

Prep time: 10 min

Cook time: 15 min

Ingredients:

- 3 tbsp olive oil
- ¼ cup onion, chopped
- 4 cloves of garlic, minced
- 1 tbsp minced ginger
- 1 cup carrots
- 1 red bell pepper, chopped
- 4 cups cauliflower rice (see basic recipes)
- 1 tbsp soy sauce
- 1 tsp sesame oil
- Salt and black pepper to taste
- Scallions for garnish

Directions:

1. Heat oil in a skillet over medium-high heat.
2. Add onion, ginger and garlic and sauté 2 minutes. Add bell pepper and carrots and cook for 3-4 minutes.
3. Add the cauliflower rice, sauces, salt and pepper and cook for another 5-6 minutes. Fluff well.
4. Taste and adjust seasonings. Serve with scallions.

Nutrition Facts Per Serving:

- Calories: 171 kcal
- Total Fat: 12.8g
- Total Carbs: 13.3g
- Dietary Fiber: 3.6g
- Net Carbs: 9.7g
- Protein: 3.41g

CAULIFLOWER KALE CURRY SOUP

Serves: 4

Prep time: 10 min

Cook time: 30 min

Ingredients:

- 4 cups cauliflower rice, uncooked (see basic recipes)
- 3 tbsp olive oil
- 1 small yellow onion, chopped
- 2 cloves garlic, minced
- 1 cup kale leaves, chopped
- 2 cups carrots, chopped
- 4 cups vegetable broth
- 1 cup coconut milk
- 3 tbsp curry powder
- ½ tsp cumin
- ½ tsp black pepper
- Salt to taste

Directions:

1. In a large pot, heat oil over medium heat.
2. Sauté minced garlic and onions until fragrant, about 3 minutes.
3. Add veggies, cauliflower rice, cumin, curry powder and black pepper and sauté 2-3 minutes.
4. Pour in the broth and coconut milk and bring to a boil. Simmer for 20 minutes.
5. Taste and add dash of salt if desired.
6. Serve.

Nutrition Facts Per Serving:

- Calories: 339 kcal
- Total Fat: 28g
- Total Carbs: 22.4g
- Dietary Fiber: 8.2g
- Net Carbs: 14.2g
- Protein: 5.18g

CREAMY BROCCOLI & CHEDDAR SOUP

Serves: 4

Prep time: 10 min

Cook time: 15 min

Ingredients:

- 1 head broccoli, cut into florets
- 2 cups vegetable broth
- 1 cup cheddar cheese, shredded
- ½ cup heavy whipping cream
- 4 tbsp butter
- ½ tsp garlic powder
- ½ tsp onion powder
- ½ tsp mustard powder
- Kosher salt and black pepper to taste

Directions:

1. Steam the broccoli florets. You can also cook them in the microwave for 4 minutes on high.
2. Blend broccoli until smooth.
3. In a pot, melt butter over medium-high heat.
4. Add the broccoli, broth, heavy whipping cream and cheese. Stir.
5. Simmer on low heat for 10 minutes.
6. Add the seasonings and serve hot.

Nutrition Facts Per Serving:

- Calories: 308 kcal
- Total Fat: 28.4g
- Total Carbs: 5.5g
- Dietary Fiber: 0.8g
- Net Carbs: 4.7g
- Protein: 9.3g

CREAMY COCONUT VEGGIE CURRY

Serves: 4

Prep time: 10 min

Cook time: 30 min

Ingredients:

- 4 cups mixed chopped vegetables (cauliflower, carrots, bell peppers, zucchini, mushrooms)
- 1 tbsp curry paste
- 2 tbsp olive oil
- 1 cup full-fat coconut cream
- 3 cups vegetable broth
- Fresh cilantro to garnish
- Cashews to garnish

Directions:

1. In a large pot, heat olive oil over medium heat.
2. Add the curry paste and cook until fragrant.

3. Add mixed vegetables and sauté for 2 minutes.
4. Pour the coconut cream and broth into the pot.
5. Bring to a boil and then simmer for 25 minutes.
6. Serve with cilantro and cashews.

Nutrition Facts Per Serving:

- Calories: 295 kcal
- Total Fat: 28.1g
- Total Carbs: 11.7g
- Dietary Fiber: 4.3g
- Net Carbs: 7.4g
- Protein: 4.46g

CHEESY ZUCCHINI GRATIN

Serves: 4

Prep time: 15 min

Cook time: 30 min

Ingredients:

- 2 tbsp butter
- 1 small onion, diced
- 2 cloves garlic, minced
- 2 medium zucchini, sliced
- 2 medium yellow squash, sliced
- 1 cup heavy cream
- 1½ cups cheese of your choice, shredded
- Salt and pepper to taste

Directions:

1. Preheat the oven to 350°F or 180°C.

2. Melt butter in a skillet and sauté onions until they appear translucent.
3. Add the minced garlic and cook for 1 minute.
4. Pour in the heavy cream and 1 cup of cheese.
5. Simmer until the sauce has thickened.
6. Grease a casserole dish.
7. Place the sliced zucchini and yellow squash in the casserole dish.
8. Gently pour the butter and cream mixture over the vegetables, and sprinkle the remaining ½ cup of cheese over the top.
9. Bake in the oven for about 30 minutes, or until the liquid has thickened and the top is golden brown.
10. Serve warm.

Nutrition Facts Per Serving:

- Calories: 371 kcal
- Total Fat: 33.68g
- Total Carbs: 5.03g
- Dietary Fiber: 0.6g
- Net Carbs: 4.43g
- Protein: 13.3g

CRUSTLESS SPINACH MUSHROOM QUICHE

Serves: 6

Prep time: 5 min

Cook time: 35 min

Ingredients:

- 10 oz frozen spinach, thawed and drained (remove as much liquid as possible)
- 2 cups mushrooms, sliced
- 6 eggs
- 1 cup heavy cream
- 1 cup mozzarella shredded
- ⅓ cup parmesan shredded
- ½ tsp garlic powder
- Salt & pepper to taste

Directions:

1. Preheat oven to 350°F.

2. Grease a pie pan.
3. Spread the drained spinach into the pan.
4. Add 1/2 cup of mozzarella cheese.
5. Next, spread mushroom.
6. In a large bowl, whisk eggs, heavy cream, parmesan, garlic powder, salt and pepper.
7. Pour the mixture in pie pan.
8. Top with the remaining of the mozzarella cheese.
9. Bake for 35-40 minutes until the top is golden brown.
10. Serve.

Nutrition Facts Per Serving:

- Calories: 195 kcal
- Total Fat: 12.24g
- Total Carbs: 6.53g
- Dietary Fiber: 2.2g
- Net Carbs: 4.33g
- Protein: 15.8g

GARLIC BASIL ZUCCHINI NOODLES

Serves: 4

Prep time: 10 min

Cook time: 10 min

Ingredients:

- 4 zucchinis, cut into noodles with a spiralizer
- 6 cloves garlic, minced
- ¼ cup fresh basil
- 6 tbsp olive oil
- 10 cherry tomatoes, halved
- 1 tsp red pepper flakes
- Salt and pepper to taste

Directions:

1. Heat olive oil in a large frying pan over medium heat.
2. Sauté garlic and red pepper flakes for 2 minutes.

3. Add zucchini noodles and sauté 3 minutes.
4. Stir in basil leaves and tomatoes, and cook for another 2 minutes.
5. Season with salt and pepper and serve.

Nutrition Facts Per Serving:

- Calories: 210 kcal
- Total Fat: 20.4g
- Total Carbs: 7.3g
- Dietary Fiber: 1g
- Net Carbs: 6.3g
- Protein: 1.3g

LOW-CARB EGGPLANT LASAGNA

Serves: 6

Prep time: 30 min

Cook time: 60 min

Ingredients:

- 1 eggplant, sliced into 10-12 thin slices
- 2 tbsp olive oil
- 3 cups marinara sauce
- 2 cups full fat ricotta cheese
- 2 cups mozzarella cheese, shredded
- 1 cup Parmesan cheese, grated
- 1 tsp dried basil
- 2 tbsp Kosher salt

Directions:

1. Lay eggplant slices on the cutting board, and

      sprinkle with salt. Leave for 20 minutes, then pat the slices dry with paper towels.

2. Preheat oven to 400°F.

3. Brush both sides of eggplant slices with olive oil and roast for 10 minutes.

4. In a bowl, mix together the ricotta cheese, 1 cup mozzarella cheese, Parmesan cheese and basil.

5. Line a baking sheet with aluminum foil.

6. Pour 1/3 of the marinara sauce into the bottom of the baking dish. Layer half of the eggplant slices.

7. Add half of the ricotta mixture and spread into an even layer.

8. Pour 1/3 of the sauce, layer the remaining eggplant and then layer the second half of the ricotta mixture.

9. Pour remaining 1 cup of sauce. Sprinkle remaining 1 cup of mozzarella cheese evenly.

10. Cover with foil and bake for 30 minutes, and then broil on high for 5 minutes.

11. Let cool 10 minutes before cutting.

Nutrition Facts Per Serving:

- Calories: 374 kcal
- Total Fat: 17g
- Total Carbs: 29g
- Dietary Fiber: 8.5g
- Net Carbs: 20.5g
- Protein: 29g

ROASTED BRUSSELS SPROUTS

Serves: 4

Prep time: 5 min

Cook time: 15 min

Ingredients:

- 20-25 Brussels sprouts, washed and stems removed
- 3 cloves garlic
- 2 tbsp olive oil
- 1 cup cream cheese
- 2 tsp fresh lemon juice
- Salt and pepper to taste

Directions:

1. In a large frying pan, heat olive oil over medium heat.

2. Add garlic and Brussels sprouts and sauté 6-8 minutes, or until tender.
3. Add cream cheese and lemon juice, and cook another 3 minutes.
4. Season with salt and pepper and serve.

Nutrition Facts Per Serving:

- Calories: 291 kcal
- Total Fat: 24.27g
- Total Carbs: 13.65g
- Dietary Fiber: 4.3g
- Net Carbs: 9.35g
- Protein: 8.25g

VEGETARIAN MEXICAN CASSEROLE

Serves: 4

Prep time: 15 min

Cook time: 30 min

Ingredients:

- 1 white onion, diced
- 2 red bell pepper, diced
- 2 green bell pepper, diced
- 1 jalapeno, diced
- 1 cup cheddar cheese, grated
- 2 tbsp olive oil
- 2 tbsp tomato paste
- 1 tsp ground cumin
- 1 tsp chili powder
- ½ tsp paprika
- ½ tsp onion powder
- ½ tsp garlic powder
- 1 tsp salt

- 1 cup salsa
- Toppings: avocado, sour cream and cilantro

Directions:

1. Preheat over to 350° F.
2. In a skillet, heat oil over medium heat.
3. Add onions, peppers, jalapeno, spices and tomato paste. Sauté for 6-8 minutes until the peppers are well cooked.
4. Coat a baking dish with cooking spray.
5. Add the veggies into baking dish.
6. Top with cheese and bake for 25-30 minutes.
7. Add salsa and toppings. Serve.

Nutrition Facts Per Serving:

- Calories: 256 kcal
- Total Fat: 18.45g
- Total Carbs: 14.63g
- Dietary Fiber: 3.2g
- Net Carbs: 11.43g
- Protein: 10.84g

ZUCCHINI & BROCCOLI SOUP

Serves: 4

Prep time: 10 min

Cook time: 40 min

Ingredients:

- 4 large zucchini
- 1 cup broccoli florets
- 2 leeks, sliced
- 1 clove garlic, minced
- 3 tbsp olive oil
- 4 cups water
- 1 cup cheddar cheese
- Salt and pepper to taste
- Parmesan cheese, for serving

Directions:

1. In a large skillet, heat oil over medium heat.

2. Sauté the leeks until transparent.
3. Add garlic, broccoli and zucchinis and sauté 5 minutes.
4. Add water, bring to a boil and then reduce heat to medium-low. Simmer for 15 minutes.
5. Blend the soup using a handheld blender until smooth.
6. Add cheddar and cook for another 3 minutes.
7. Add parmesan cheese and serve.

Nutrition Facts Per Serving:

- Calories: 313 kcal
- Total Fat: 22.53g
- Total Carbs: 18.4g
- Dietary Fiber: 4.5g
- Net Carbs: 13.9g
- Protein: 13.1g

SNACK RECIPES

CHEESY FRIED EGGPLANT

Serves: 6

Prep time: 10 min

Cook time: 10 min

Ingredients:

- 1 eggplant, cut into thin slices
- 1 egg
- ½ cup butter
- 1 cup almond flour
- 1 cup Parmesan cheese, grated
- ½ tsp garlic powder
- ½ tsp onion powder
- Salt and pepper to taste

Directions:

1. On a plate, arrange the eggplant slices and sprinkle with salt. Let sit for 20 minutes.

2. In a small bowl, mix Parmesan cheese, garlic powder, onion powder, almond flour, salt and pepper.
3. In another bowl, whisk the egg.
4. Heat butter in a frying pan over medium heat.
5. Dip an eggplant slice in the egg, then in the flour mixture. Fry until golden brown. Repeat until all the eggplant slices are fried.
6. Drain excess oil with paper towels.
7. Serve.

Nutrition Facts Per Serving:

- Calories: 254 kcal
- Total Fat: 21.9g
- Total Carbs: 8.6g
- Dietary Fiber: 2.9g
- Net Carbs: 5.7g
- Protein: 7.5g

EASY KETO ICE CREAM

If you don't have cream of tartar, you can use a ¼ teaspoon of apple cider vinegar, and you can easily turn this dairy free by using coconut milk which will work just as well for this sweet and simple recipe.

Serves: 1

Prep time: 10 min

Total time: 30 min

Ingredients:

- 4 large eggs
- ¼ tsp cream of tartar
- ½ cup erythritol
- 1¼ cup heavy whipping cream
- 1 tbsp vanilla extract

Directions:

1. Start by separating your egg yolks from your egg whites, and whisk the egg whites with the cream of tartar. The egg whites will begin to thicken, and as they do you're going to need to add the Erythritol. They should start to form stiff peaks, and you'll need to keep whisking until they do.

2. Take another bowl, and start to whisk your cream. Soft peaks should start to form as the whisk is removed, but you'll need to be careful not to over whisk the cream.

3. In a third bowl, combine your egg yolks with the vanilla.

4. Now you can fold the whisked egg whites into the now whipped cream.

5. Add in your egg yolk mixture, and continue to gently fold with a spatula until thoroughly combined.

6. Place it in a pan, preferably a loaf pan, and let it sit. All hands on time is done, but it'll need to sit for about two hours.

Nutrition Facts Per Serving:

- Calories: 238 kcal
- Total Fat: 22.2g
- Total Carbs: 2.3g
- Dietary Fiber: 0g
- Net Carbs: 2.3g
- Protein: 5.1g

GUACAMOLE

Serves: 4

Prep time: 10 min

Cook time: 0 min

Ingredients:

- 2 avocados, peeled and pit
- 4 grape tomatoes, finely diced
- ½ small red onion, finely diced
- Juice of ½ lime
- 1 tbsp olive oil
- 1 clove garlic, minced
- Fresh cilantro, chopped
- Salt and pepper to taste

Directions:

1. In a mixing bowl, mash the avocados.
2. Add the tomatoes and onions into the bowl.

3. Add the olive oil, garlic, lime juice, cilantro to the mixture.
4. Season with salt and pepper and serve.

Nutrition Facts Per Serving:

- Calories: 205 kcal
- Total Fat: 18.15g
- Total Carbs: 12g
- Dietary Fiber: 7g
- Net Carbs: 5g
- Protein: 2.44g

KALE CHIPS

Serves: 2

Prep time: 10 min

Cook time: 5 min

Ingredients:

- 3 tsp of olive oil
- 12 pieces of kale leaves
- Salt and pepper, as needed

Directions:

1. Preheat oven to 350°F or 175°C.
2. Line a baking sheet with parchment paper.
3. Wash and thoroughly dry kale leaves and place them on the baking sheet.
4. Drizzle kale with olive oil and sprinkle with salt and pepper.
5. Bake 10 to 15 minutes.

6. Serve.

Nutrition Facts Per Serving:

- Calories: 107 kcal
- Total Fat: 7.64g
- Total Carbs: 8.4g
- Dietary Fiber: 3.5g
- Net Carbs: 4.9g
- Protein: 4.11g

VEGAN COCONUT VANILLA ICE CREAM

Serves: 6

Prep time: 10 min

Cook time: 0 min

Ingredients:

- 2 cups full-fat coconut cream
- ¼ cup erythritol, or sweetener of your choice
- 2 tsp vanilla extract
- Pinch of salt

Directions:

1. In a large bowl, stir together all the ingredients.
2. Pour the mixture in ice cube trays and freeze until frozen.
3. Thaw slightly and blend the frozen cubes in a blender.
4. Serve.

Nutrition Facts Per Serving:

- Calories: 296 kcal
- Total Fat: 27.8g
- Total Carbs: 12.5g
- Dietary Fiber: 1.8g
- Net Carbs: 10.7g
- Protein: 2.9g

PARMESAN CHIPS

Serves: 4

Prep time: 10 min

Cook time: 15 min

Ingredients:

- 6 oz grated Parmesan cheese
- 4 tbsp almond flour
- 1 tsp rosemary
- ½ tsp garlic powder

Directions:

1. Start by heating your oven to 350°F or 180°C.
2. Mix Parmesan cheese and almond flour in a medium bowl.
3. Add rosemary and garlic powder, and continue to mix everything together.

4. Place each tablespoon of cheese mixture on a baking sheet.
5. Bake for 10-15 minutes.
6. Let cool before serving.

Nutrition Facts Per Serving:

- Calories: 227 kcal
- Total Fat: 16g
- Total Carbs: 8g
- Dietary Fiber: 1g
- Net Carbs: 7g
- Protein: 13.9g

PEANUT BUTTER COOKIE

Serves: 12

Prep time: 15 min

Cook time: 10 min

Ingredients:

- 1 cup peanut butter
- ½ cup powdered erythritol
- 1 egg

Directions:

1. Preheat oven to 350°F or 175°C.
2. In a medium bowl, combine the peanut butter, erythritol and the egg. Mix well.
3. Form the cookie dough into 1-inch balls.
4. Place the balls on a parchment paper lined baking sheet.
5. Press down on a dough with a fork twice in

opposite directions. Repeat with the rest of the doughs.

6. Bake for about 12 minutes.
7. Let cool for 5 minutes before serving.

Nutrition Facts Per Serving:

- Calories: 80 kcal
- Total Fat: 5.12g
- Total Carbs: 7.46g
- Dietary Fiber: 1.5g
- Net Carbs: 5.96g
- Protein: 2.91g

PEANUT BUTTER FUDGE

Serves: 10

Prep time: 5 min

Cook time: 10 min

Ingredients:

- 1 cup unsweetened peanut butter
- 1 cup coconut oil
- 1 tsp vanilla extract
- 1 tbsp heavy whipping cream
- Optional: desired sugar substitute to taste

Directions:

1. Line a square pan with parchment paper.
2. In a microwave-safe bowl, melt peanut butter and coconut oil in the microwave.
3. Add the rest of the ingredients and stir well.

4. Add the mixture to your blender and blend until smooth.
5. Pour the mixture into the pan. Spread out evenly.
6. Refrigerate until set, about 2 hours.

Nutrition Facts Per Serving:

- Calories: 224 kcal
- Total Fat: 22.5g
- Total Carbs: 5.4g
- Dietary Fiber: 0.4g
- Net Carbs: 5g
- Protein: 1.54g

STRAWBERRY CHEESECAKE MINIS

Serves: 8

Prep Time: 5 min

Total Time: 15-20 min

Ingredients:

- ½ cup strawberries, fresh & mashed
- ¾ cup cream cheese, softened
- ¼ cup coconut oil, softened
- 10-15 drops liquid stevia
- 1 tsp vanilla extract

Directions:

1. Start by combining all of the ingredients in a bowl, and mixing with a hand mixer until completely smooth. You can also do this in a high-speed blender.
2. Spoon into mini muffin tins, and place in the

freezer. It'll take about two hours to set, and then you can place them in the fridge.

Nutritional Facts per Serving:

- Calories: 129 kcal
- Total Fat: 13.27g
- Total Carbs: 1.55g
- Dietary Fiber: 0.2g
- Net Carbs: 1.35g
- Protein: 1.66g

AFTERWORD

You made it to the end. Congratulations! I would like to thank you again for reading my book and starting the Vegetarian Ketogenic journey. I hope that the information I provided in this book is helpful and you have found everything you need.

Being a vegetarian and being in ketosis is not easy, but if you stick to the diet, and consume only clean and whole food, you will soon see the amazing results.

All the best for your future!

AUTHOR'S NOTE

Thank you so much for taking the time to read my book. I hope you have enjoyed reading this book as much as I've enjoyed writing it. If you enjoyed this book, please consider leaving a review on Amazon. Your support really means a lot and keeps me going.

If you have any questions, please don't hesitate to contact me at ask@cleaneatingspirit.com

Don't forget to follow me on Facebook and Instagram for more information related to health and wellness.

Facebook: https://www.facebook.com/cleaneatingspirit/

Instagram: https://www.instagram.com/cleaneatingspirit

Made in the USA
Middletown, DE
05 December 2018